Astroturfing
for
Spring

ASTROTURFING
for
SPRING

D.J. Huppatz

PUNCHER & WATTMANN

First published in 2021
Published by Puncher and Wattmann
PO Box 279
Waratah NSW 2298

http://www.puncherandwattmann.com
puncherandwattmann@bigpond.com

NATIONAL
LIBRARY
OF AUSTRALIA

A catalogue entry for this book is available from the National Library of Australia.

ISBN   9781925780932

Cover design by Miranda Douglas
Typesetting by Morgan Arnett
Printed by Lightning Source International

Contents

Excess Keratin

Mars was just an excuse.
The whole thing about cratering
is dead, though pedants are still
tempted by dents in the crust.
The discovery of another late
surviving population of Neanderthals
only proves that celebrities who ruin
themselves with plastic surgery
will eventually become potpourri.
So, don't discard your yo-yo,
be consistent with your marriages
and the distant Oort cloud will
continue to oust weakly bound bodies.
Do I need to repeat any of this?

Presumably, some vanished in the Pacific
before they reached Easter Island, maybe
they met some other Hobbits on the way
back from a daytrip to Bali. But just
because you shave your hairy back and
get around in leather yoga pants do you
really think slicing open autistic mice brains
might control the tidal forces from the disk
and bulge of the Milky Way? Seriously?
By all means keep returning to the Neander Valley
looking for a cure for your allergies but I know
one day the Vaporous steam of the Fire Spirit
will lead us to the place of the Miraculous Well.
I still can't believe we lost Pluto.

Everybody Knows What the Score Is

I

10 sentences about favourite patisseries.
I am not real, please don't touch me.

An emu running wild in New Hampshire.
Emunah means faithlessness.
Meaning witness.

Are we all related or what?

II

Four pairs of herons, Madagascan
vanilla cream clouds forming letters.
First I saw SCARE, then it turned into SCORE.
Didn't you see it?

Later I realized there's a mysterious
handsome stranger living in my head.

The Insect Drive

Dripping clinic zone or ozone
the altar smoked red and apple-
wood chips bled decimal excess.
Capital edited the moan. When
will Syria change your crisis?

The procedure hurt like a signal
given a shadow, a half-jerk with a
new name. Queues form for more.
Surplus wings, amphibious things,
hear the hooves of awesome horses.

Lower the chandeliers, refill your
cosmetic holes with polyamory.
Hold the sphere volunteers, bow low,
calculate a paradise beyond the ethic
horizon. This gnome riots, alone.

My memory sings in wild analogue,
an uncompromising squint and a
cache named The Insect Drive.
Dry roasted singly, each sound
crisp. Desire cracks the sky.

Your Zoloft is Making Me Soft

Hey, listen up! I was all Mirth when the nymphs
checked out and someone cut the coke with Plan B.

The better Latins toasted pottery shards and spoke plainly
while Mr Trippy and Les Belles sang "All the Irony in Heaven".

If you must keep posting funeral selfies, said the Latins,
employ Counterfactual Regret Minimization
and deadpool that ancient astronaut theory.

Luckily, my obscurantist hypnosis practice
was starting to totally literature it and I could finally
afford to move to the Magical Land of Hedge Funds.

Behold, Astringent Father, beyond the chicken-proof
brick fence running the length of Separation Street,
Carbon Derivatives, slippery as verbs in compression pants.

Behold, Sweet Jane, beyond the vaporous steam that
saturates High Street in day-glo luminosity, a blossoming
oasis of lonely poets studying the rules of verse.

Look around the night sky for a star that's flashy, sang Mr Trippy,
signs of secret clouds, the cherub Contemplation aloft.

O Astrum, vision of firm corrugations, your icing
is so lickable but your Zoloft is making me soft.

Trickle

When Boo Boo Kitty loosened the calculating screw,
a trickle-down figment of her imagination widened on
the glass outside. Poetry pools face severe penalties so
the board now generates a greater percentage of lyrical
buzz in order to use linguistic resources more efficiently.

Not accidently, whatever stories boxed in clauses of fair trade
wallet punctuation within processes meant I could only create
three more shadow doppelgangers before the planned expressway
banned my barn raising. Don't worry, says Boo Boo, here's
a piece of nervous tissue to clean up your synaptic discharge.

Suspended on beyond, mono trifling rightness got lost
in the blinding light of a generic deity. Someone started
stripping the ownership lining but the data compression
was already complete. Pass the popcorn, said Boo Boo,
you can choose whatever algorithms turn you on.

Ad hoc microscopic matter that cannot participate faced the
looming terminology deadline then fell into a binary heap.
Trickles untie advanced ideas that inspire celestial navigation.
Luckily Boo Boo plumbed into another management strategy:
One day my fountain will come, I will bubble up.

But the gates never opened. A pomp of winning Graces
caught the rising silicone tide and Kitty was left behind
to clean up the cream. Where are the coasts of light?
Drinking from my bottle of aspirations, I am weary
of colouring within the lines of this goldfish refrain.

A tickle widens the seams, impressions in gravy
etched in dust lame faith studies the inside of a fury.
If you prefer the density of a dot to a relative bubble
we can recalibrate your complaint. When the sales
started, Boo Boo was drenched in Elysian dew.

Between noun pulses you need to get down to the doing,
even when the dripping starts blocking your image track.
App logs support each portable premise but the trick is
template modification to avoid figurative stickiness:
reflections on the surface flow are all you need to know.

The shockwave from the supernova is approaching the Pillars
of Creation: adjust your receptors, assemble the crystals.
After the social life of small screens Kitty peels off her wings
smooths out the wrinkles in time, yet glycerine tears trickle
onto the red carpet as she tweets bees bees bees bees bees.

Reaching Out

Hello, I am currently 15 years old and I want to become a walrus. I know there's a million people out there just like me, but I promise you, I'm different. On December 15th, I'm moving to Antarctica, home of the greatest walruses. I've already cut off my arms, and now slide on my stomach everywhere I go as training. I may not be a walrus yet, but I promise you if you give me a chance and the support I need, I will become the greatest walrus ever. If you have any questions or maybe advice, just inbox me. Thanks so much.

I'm Just Glad the Airbag Deployed

Something, something, meow meow beans.
Swallowing crash plastic panic, it's time
to self-actualize a time before Pantone blue.
Unfashionable utopia, as used by last year's
worn leggings. Then Kalam fell down.

Unsame polyester swirl hair over
shelled eyes the sunrise chose a
meanwhile leaf embedded with yawn.
We weeded Villa d'Smug so straw-
berries might jam up cupboards to come.

Lycra wordplay in the psalms bin,
spooling volume from singular
to seeding. Adjust the sun. Push
button suspended on beyond. At
alive. This day isn't going away.

Every hear afixed with twists
already installed, as table is
already a diminutive form of tablet.
Meow scratches next to something.
As the gods vibe on a leaf drop.

When will the word defect below air?
Peer at the screen in the hope of finding
magic among maze beans. The chorus
flowers. My windmill mind has a cause.
This air here. Therefore semaphore.

Keep pointing at immaterial phenomena,
like winter. An elegy leaked colours into
the cracks, sealing in inertia. Edge words
irritate then clot the machine. Beware
empty Tupperware, there is no or there.

Beans contain imagery that may concern
some readers: a source of chorus flowers
represses lust for releasing mist. Circuitry
misprints as the mask tightens and sticky
words can't undo incomplete pollination.

Watch What Happens Next

I

Someone in a blue shirt walking away
gets blurred. Am poet. Can confirm.

This fruit is defective, it doesn't sing.
Maybe "decorative" isn't the right term.

You find one dagger and a cabbage. Thanks
for circling, I totally would've missed that.

Beyond detection, bending from clouds,
his dollars wander as the earth goes flat.

II

When your feed is full of couples on
honeymoon doing cooking classes

it's like real life. But better. All I see
is people not wearing safety glasses.

Then tiresome prophets debate sustainable
syntax until they settle on a suitable text.

Did you save the changes? Did you not
WATCH WHAT HAPPENS NEXT?

Why Mess With Perfection?

Lip fillers and spray tanned realness
only add to the perfect over-allness
of another agent not calling day. A
bleached array let glory through.

Why deny the defacer? Sounds like
it's time to bring out the heart-shaped
glitter confetti and reflect upon the
high-tech low-carb life you chose.

We should save our frozen embryos
just in case carbon-based biological
neural networks inside a cranium start
working out better than shadow-people,

before the true exchange of rainbow
lip bit cuteness silences the trending
feedback group with an oogle glut.
I hope your day is as nice as my butt.

Pipeline

A bubbler disruption: no one
wants to eat the blame cookie.
Gold magnitudes in a hollow collar,
something collides with something else

in a large collider, capillaries branching
against objective stock along the line.
Fake skin bitmap skips but doesn't fret
about what's happening down-stream.

Punctuated by columns, the temple's tube
fogs the screen. Before you judge another
glue, test the water. Our certified connector
is spitting pips below the Damascus volcano.

We should schedule more on-screen variance
during the next strategic surf reef bounce and
pipe outside the lines. Florentine eggs drip
mustard seeds. Forget the swallow overflow.

Conjured from breakfast, distant violence
smells like innovation. Amid worn glory,
outsourced hope pulps exposure only to
duct tape over poor portfolio decisions. A

moving mathematics generalizes goodbye
so everyone's happy across the three horizons.
And so are you, until your hazard suit springs
a leak then test rust cheats press skills refresh.

Leaked light is absorbed into a loop-
hole as long as the river inside you is
first past the fist pump. The remainder
reverts to motion – smoke flakes, tar sands.

An acoustic spike in the telescopic circuitry,
each improving, state after state they gain,
gathering loose overtones, each bubbling
detain reform deform detonation refrain.

The Angel's Share

An extract gathers an opus: the bass
drop of heaven's deep organ blow oaks
at the expanse. Rejoice O humble grass
as sunlight scrolls across dissonant continents –
silver foiled clouds wrap, warp and swallow,
far from empty foyers. Great chords crease
the shore. Even after the decay into
quarks, our glasses are still ringing.

An exhaustive algorithm rattles, overspills
on a stony beach. Angels burble long
sentences into our shell-shaped receptors.
In this smoky stillness, figures in peat
animate sensible objects. Beam, O obsolete
breath, beam on the earth's shadow as ice
works its way backwards despite the unity of
minds above the Mind, minds with dry feet.

Hipster Beards Vs. Momcore Hiking Realness

So stop hating kale chips indefinite articles unshopped photos
put the laundry basket down there's a quaint bearded diversion
at the door of my Thornbury stoop party. The vintage fridge
hums every time we blow pints of craft into the quinoa salad.

Outdoors he chopped down trees when the streets ran red with
plaid then something happened when you were folding laundry or
slow roasting poetry when Brunswick was Bushwick pocketing
the picture-world of a myriad interrupting upcycling cacti.

Thumbs up for Schopenhauer's objection to the cosmological argument.
Thumbs up for riding a low rider to new lowness.
Thumbs up for momcore hiking realness.

You've probably never heard of the thread in question but what's
left of life is a low-budget utopia measured out in champagne flutes
cut into Blank Frame pieces of an inverted matrix come women
gather into this true space this spherical crucible for middling.

Chocolate fudge edge sheds price tag eddies around
sculpted nails and corrugations on an ungendered sippy cup
since the nymphs bailed up the fame ramp we use the smudge
tool on the couch these stuck on antlers will recharge your smile.

Is that really a Biggie Smalls print on her yoga pants?
Is this really a safe place to collect crockpot dip recipes?
Is this really just another tale of blonde triumph?

That's panic hanging from your rear-vision mirror Lululemon Mom
and I know the latest lamentation update was difficult to thrift
so why even try to plaster over the lost decades listening to vinyl
poetry jams – I bet those headphones aren't even plugged in.

Outside the big box look it's moms who don't even know
they're moms drinking artisanal rum like it's Havana singing "my
problems were a mountain and I was the solution" and though
I know I should've swiped left Defeatism is not my Friendster.

Add colour to uninhabited atmospheres.
Add badass whiskey dadness.
Add Hadrian as the original hipster.

In the pumice lounge, Renaissance Mom poses next to Hipster Beards
as inflation slows and fans of clogs barter for food truck haircuts but I'm
always one move behind in the Zumba class that is I can wear a sequined
llama sweater hand made in Bolivia but I'll never be badass like dad.

So just go with wake and bake, post-momcore while it's still available in jam
jars, before the extras from a Civil War documentary descend, look there's
me in a knitted beanie chewing a wheat-stalk and while we're dropping
truth bombs I like not having to worry about being eaten by larger creatures.

A Guide to Selfing

1. *Feed your Self*

Forget appleseed do-gooders, spreading splendid cotton, this is my
breakfast on white bedsheets morning. This is my freshly pressed
family sweatshop pic, my freshly pressed green (you probably haven't
heard of it) protein shake. This is a Process that is born alive almost
continuously through conditioned states and typewriter poems on
reclaimed timber. I can even do it without the aid of pollen vectors if
you pass me another Slender Blend.

2. *Put your Self first*

There's some backstage drama going on with the Five Aggregates of
Attachment, something about a sponsor. Rag gangs who meet at the
river for a minimum wage riot are not number one. You know bespoke
tacos won't wait, so maybe we should go straight for the self-saucing
orchid pudding truck. All these Stories of Rumination are starting to
sound the same.

3. *Adorn Your Self*

Be a rainbow. Persist, it's only morning. Juicy shampoo embeds
circuitry that opens to enable the flow. Now work that wig like Louis
XIV. Ah-ha — you know who!

4. *Take some Self time*

All day happy hour wasn't edgy enough to improve our Well Being
so I set retouch on autopilot for a while. Su Jin was a Buddhist and a
vegetarian, but that did not stop him from drinking wine and having a
good time. Scroll down, you deserve it.

winky face

so much depends
upon

an inkling
this

little ink is
so cute

aww...
panda hug!

From Poetry to English

according to google, compact
storage devices sometimes
deviate into meaning ducts.

basketball-orange flavour
doesn't have the same dense
buzz as storm of pollen does.

though many angels disagree,
remiss graphic blocks are often
"roughly synonymous" with reality.

it's possible all this is true, but
you'd be better off power walking
around the mall without me.

America

I

As the beach retreats, America
runs on happy clams and new
ways to make asparagus shine.
Drugged by freedom, bare spears
have become offensive to many.
They clearly need a new strategy.

I follow a lot of dogs. Now that
I'm the bonus policy holder for
the spiritual insurance of three
perfect angels, I need the pillar of
faith that only a pocket chihuahua
dressed as Marie Antoinette provides.

The threesome between stars, stripes
and cheese doodles in the parking lot
of a shuttered Dollar General roughly
equals the number of bald eagles killed
each year by wind turbines. Who knew?
These days, everybody wants choices.

II

Mine eyes have seen blessed trailer parks
fringing southern cities, peanut butter
cups and flavoured detox tea. Now I'm
hungry. Stars nest in the strip mall
by sugar-free gummy bears in maternity
dresses. I too twirl for three-way chili.

Inhabiting abattoirs, accelerating over the
wilted earth or masturbating quietly with the
lights out, you forgot to crush the serpent
under your heel. Seriously America, what's
up with you? Sharing atoms like we do,
I think dark matter is just an excuse.

I'm sick of hunting for bookstores,
confident, mystical, naked. America,
when my socialist algorithm infects
your sensorial location devices, corn
won't save you. And just so you know,
my fifteen minutes isn't up just yet.

Pacman

I

May God bless the country
you are helping to punctuate.
Oh. My. Squash.
Sliced white bread.
No jeans for refugees. And the week
before, 27 368 photos of the sea
(her hotel window view)
and her salads. Now STOP
validating my genetic lottery.

Nom nom.
Unblocked rows
of Tiffany jewellery
now on freeview.

Now even newer.

II

Picasso's Guernica really speaks to me.
It represents the civil war in my soul.

Start deleting grievers.
Start adding cats.

But what's the difference
between a ghost and a griever?

There are no funds available
to answer this question.

My mother was a eugenic
experiment. Nom nom confirms it.
Imagine power pellets are seashells
and there are no borders in this maze.

Zombies can pop up anywhere.
Even on a clean-eating blog.

Do You Feel Me?

Whatever interconnects people
want for concealing meaning
without any above-your-head
commentary on the dullness of
existence just arrived at another
layer of dramatic puppet realness
perpetually retreating towards
Hallmark card happiness:

*I hope Greenland melts. It's
a miserable place to live.*

This is not a useful gardening
tool or Himalayan songbook.
I mean this thing dumps
like a truck. Truck. Truck.

A Very Big Dust Cloud

A bump
in the "arrangement" of the whole thing
and hydrogen atoms clump together like
Aloo Tikki, shelled peas, blood-splattered trees.
That's when I first got that mini fist bump
feeling, gyrating around a thought-post,
fresh from witless semiosis, dissolving
a lump of garam masala in distilled spit.

Do you remember
how long we waited
for the next star to blow up?

Well that
was a painful chain and I'm just not feeling
the group buzz anymore. If we could only
uncloud this browser and see these undivided
motes stumbling towards the Andromeda merger,
worlds wrought through calculating the food miles
of cappuccinos as our beam of warm imagination stays
spongy on the inside, crisp-crusted on the outside.

Most people
are just waiting
for the giveaways.

Ghoogle

O roof shoots off-stage an
engineer fetches me umbrella
drinks: one less herring to ouch.

I'm a chicken nugget dressed
with cloud (miscalled "puff")
typo squatting in oyster folds.

No more carbon or no more
turbulent eruption of air (you
do not want to open that can).

As an imperfect actor in front
of a green screen I think it's
time to lower the chandelier.

It's the Corona and lime my friends.
It makes me fucking Shakespeare.

We Are All Out of Progress

I

I listened to Proverbs on my commute
and I believe this captures nicely what

Beyoncé is saying, surfing all that Good
Good and giving prudence to the simple.

During the first tribal council, my heart,
skinned to internal decimals, spurned all

auto-correct. I can't believe I now have to
login to avoid bad company, discharging trails

of tokens through this straw-built citadel fringed with
strip club curtains. Didn't Wisdom leave a message?

Heart says *yes*, horoscope says *no* so I dipped
my potato chips in a dip called *Despair*.

II

Wait, was that our congealed future, back there,
somewhere? That protein looked good on you.

Her lyrical theorem bubble lifted the wallpaper, too
much figurative stickiness is disguised as percent.

So the swallow escaped to air shaped in waves,
her tattoo reminds me of my childhood, her lips

of meaning ducts that shelter homeless phrases.
How many poems ago did we hear this already?

Don't worry, I'll hook you up with my guy at infinity
mirror emporium. Good Good glitched so we used the Tarot

to predict when the lamp of the wicked will get snuffed out.
The rising tide of bleached selfies will lift our boat.

A Classical Remainder

Hope dodges skinned property. A
reduction in spiritual expenditure
imposed this brickness around the
central loneliness model. Does the
metric permit a classical remainder?

In fawn pelts past we would
take a knife to the lyrics while
the plain-spoken remained safe
behind national palings. Now
a trusted associate persuades
the hello in wrong. There's a
pot of gold at the end, he says,
after you peel off the rainbow
layers. Hope warms to the lie.

My Lawn is Green

The old punctuation – fence meets fence – is
gone. Now choose the background that best
represents you: plum blossom or plum laurels
will win the last Home Renovator Revolution.

I'm learning how to toss salad: flavour rages
under the lettuce, a carrot disappears like a
vascular access device insertion. Lawn owners
water their concrete avatars with tears.

Ask my secretary to manage the conflicting
schedules of pink plastic flamingos, pull up
the blinds and witness their demise but remember
only lawful desires are allowed on the lawn.

Vote for skin that bounces back like it used to.
Exploit the asterisk over the sat nav system.
Wait, are you astroturfing for her? Ugg bling
ugg's on the other foot now isn't it, sock puppet.

Why Won't This Anthology Overflow?

Hedged against age, the enclosed fire
works are part of your incentive package.
Please tell me "custard" is code for
something. Your Calvin Kleins are
leaking metrics from a collapsing star:
what does *that* mean, Astrogirl?

This conversation has nothing to do with
automated image rhetoric or computers that
determine user characteristics assessment.
We should create a blossoming oasis of
self-realization, preserved with the Spice
of the First Intellect. When the old men
finally stop fly fishing from the bleachers
we can get rid of *Lorem Ipsum* forever.

Nature Unplugged

Thy land, compacted to the slack,
no word is firm. Arcadia's damp
heart-thong shot juiced my
idle residue – being Greek
yoghurt isn't what it used to be.

Every time I spread pine straw,
amoebas sing, corrupting acorns.
I see you've spray-tanned your
perpetually beige Self – so many
professional friends are doing it.

Gentle Sequel, please delete this
squandered option. Abounding
ampersands suppress panic as
syllables scroll more serotonin.

On the Rocks

Yes, this place. Its crescent-shape
lured mercantile bonding confetti on
scales dried from a long journey.

Improving with age, said the landlord.

Unstories haul away before Francis Greenway's
classical symmetry: fresh mistress of shameless
April keeled on a gust then bricked our daily bread
in warehouse courtyards fitted with cordial planters.

Walkable tourism cultivates admiration for poverty.

Comes comfort and contrivance where HOPE
once stood and waved his mop thrum hair,
where a stick beat the Tank Stream Tune
– *equal charm equal joy* – though
too many crooked trees stood in the way.

Bitumen is a good cover, said the governor.

Seeding, breeding and geocaching: according
to the latest algorithm, we are still shelving
convictions here. Fresh off the boat, striking measures
by way of laws *designed to civilize*. So were we still
gittin civil when we hit on that mound of birdshit
in the Pacific? Perhaps some streets can't be straightened.

And we're still here, dancing in a retro forest of soundproof wallpaper we just had installed below the Cahill Expressway. Fudge follows fudge to try and explain it all away and join in the chorus of the Formerly Pleasant Island theme song.

Hey! Look out for the bombora, said Bennelong.

I Notice Someone Left Crumbs on the Balcony

I

If you like the moon or
any other really big rock
you're gonna *love* my
asteroid stars and the
story of how I got them.

II

Before binomials, names
of plants in books were just
words strung together. Kids
with kites are not evidence
that spring has finally arrived.

III

People are freaking out
about this Japanese woman
with pigeon shoes. I heard
she lives in a giant green
house and never goes out.

Men With Selfish Centres

On the outskirts of one of the Milky Way's
spiral arms, massively parallel POWER7
processors shaped a silhouette and everyone
knows what happens next: I couldn't get
into modelling so got a job collecting urine
for algorithms. Now I know how shepherds
felt when fences put them out of business.

Across the fuss, a corridor rolls onto another
corridor, then onto the freeway. Bundles of
selfish energies populate this fictional bit-
map, plain men in plain suits, men with
selfish centres driving biblical machines in
seemingly unstoppable motion. We have
spare fear stashed at the next stop, they say.

Once the data was released, we were angry
at the boggle of decimal excess, the worlds
wrought in cabling, the best red velvet cake
possible from all permutations. Our ghosting
awareness training alerted us to his thin white
skin, tanned flat as an icon. The Quran says
that a spider's web makes the frailest home.

Elsewhere (not at all plain build), the name-
less 3.6 billion looked for food but got warm,
salted coral. Heat becomes bone, marrow, meds.
Where am I placed in this congested race into the
unknown unknown? Underneath this anatomy
there's a jaded old avatar weighed down with
each pulse of unfunded cosmic consciousness.

Erotic robots have already sniffed which way
the wind is blowing, old fashioned pattern
recognition won't cut it anymore and the
next lubricant shortage could see them back
in the fields picking strawberries. Thankfully,
aesthetic sensibility is not essential. Farming
and gardening are not the same as astronomy.

Alternative Facts, Bad Luck and Bad Timing
left us with an Amateur Hour Adobe After
Effects background overlaid with images of women
cradling babies in the ruins of a city in the Middle
East. Mostly there are too many pulses to process,
too much acid-wash rhetoric. Not even my grooming
accessory can make up for the absence of poetry.

Bright

Last night burnt a hole in today,
my face creased at the leaf debris
it caught. Stop looking for where
the when began. Even willows know.

Placed in hereness, Mt Buffalo,
still smouldering at the edges.

One leafs, to imitate and sedate
a cropped vision. Thus sounding.

Moths cough from the mount's orbit
on top of a composite, speakers don't
reveal their sources. The river in a choke-
hold, Mt. Buffalo wraps a disappearing.

Deepening on speed, leaving is over:
purges age here without remainder.

On the Ovens

Suppose a sequence of evens – staying
the same others and water flows, slips
on hold, on align. Ribs of tobacco kilns
reappear as wine labels, mountains as
outlines of commotion. Unfixed, the
edges are dissolving in the missing.

On the contours of a flood, cod could.
An unknown Bangerung man fixed on
a postcard, posed with his canoe. My
uttering drifts and sticks in the hope
that the firmament be firm again after
surplus management, posed on the clog.

Some worry about clog but

                    clog doesn't wash the chop.

Suppose we summon the serpent's head, kindle
the bark to a tolerable heat, lead the chop chop
retreat onto the screen and brew the hops gold?

On the Torryong, digging holes at the edge of
a lagoon. Here come the blackberries – one sun
uprolled the whole and down came another one.

Tweening

So you're feeling the pinch
around your percent, its shape
doesn't fire on most of the clicks.
I listen to transmissions when my app
meters appropriate Bodily Organs
into Ozone Champagne. Can
the turtle mend this subroutine?

Everyone abused in Helvetica
is entitled to jingling rhymes.
A single nimble origin, unfit digit,
vaporous steam of the Fire Spirit.

If quarks really do cause inflation,
Honey Badger don't care. Looks like
she's on the verge. Like, THE VERGE.

What's Nature Complaining About This Time?

Not a ripple on the wine-dark paving this morning,
data projection schemes reconfigured the sky as
Truth dropped on my head. Bird is a bright word.

We supply information on population and we know
you want to know more about lol so true and haha.
We have storage solutions, so why won't nature smile?

I'm recycling prefab futures into fashionable utopias:
this one's called The Dictatorship of Things. Birch trees
and snow-covered mountains are available in poster-size.

Hey Spotted Treefrog, I know buds are slow but we're
franchising new branches so now you can get the energy
discounts you're entitled to. We're struggling for you!

Let the folk and their flocks in the fields be jubilant!
Let the mean number of calling males rise!
Let the seed the sower sowed at last be seen!

Why do you think the Higgs Boson is shaped like a
cross? Aerosol poetry only brings forth thistles and
thorns: why not order another dozen roses? I'm tired

of being God's glitch on Earth now this one
is rapidly deflating. Don't worry Kermit,
I saved you an heirloom purple carrot.

Swells

Written in meadows, wrung breath, marks
made in the riveting. Data, wrought from
puffballs levelling up into thin air, won't
manage Arcadia's cancer. An iron bridge
facilitates efficient communications
on every romantic answering service,
even when weighed down by padlocks.

A light mask removes a nipple. Floods
over the bowl simulate Time's Differential
going bareback, cracked, unconnected and
leaking in radio bursts. An interrupt screen
script overload swells until its over-swollen.
Such fear. So much wine and shoe shine
so much soda sop-logged to first slime.

On Sovereign Hill

I

After they replaced my chip, the
storms of obstruction cleared and
computational submission, in all its
bits and sweats, twilled this shaping
space into a golden bathroom mirror.

High on Adderall, I named myself
Proteus yet dollars kept migrating
to the next lifestyle hustle. So,
in order to gain further exposure,
I stopped sleeping with the seals.

My cup was mostly empty and even
Siri mistook my breadcrumbs of love
for rhetorical litter within which (and
she doesn't know this) – one day –
miracles might yet grow. All that

because Paterson was so boring,
we simply drove straight through.
Let's not pretend we're looking
for an authentic accommodation
experience or a flower of the day.

II

After they replaced my chip, I didn't
feel like a city anymore. It's easy to
pigeonhole yourself so it was a great
relief to know that even lizards have
low dopamine levels sometimes.

Inside myself there are several selves
nostalgic for giant robots on Pentagon
contracts so we stopped for lunch in
Rivendell to watch scruffy paradigms
fold into wiggly hills and valleys.

So many matches made me want to
set things on fire but we can't cross the
blood barrier. Don't ditch venture booty
she replied with a gurgle. Autonomous
things are easily mistaken for poetry.

Rivendell was pretty cosmopolitan, but
had nothing of the sea, not even a decent
waterfall. I cranked up the "creativity"
output and painted the bathroom Burble
Simp. That should dissolve our binary.

In Brooklyn

A bagel enlightened my morning
after truth marched past the stoop

These shoes won't shine anymore
Those tattoos, condensed therapy

Along Fulton, I'm digging bubbles
and ghosts, and when it's hot I'm

Super Fudge Chunk humming on
diner coffee and rusted rivets a

vocal overflow schmearing inter-
pretation on an East River flux

raising an opus of artisanal donuts
forested in pretzel-smoked books

These furrows of mourning, a gift of pain
Those dreams, a gift of polished memory

It's addictive, this quality of felt vibes
razzed and jazzed in activated space so

I'm dragging and clicking my way to
the subway in cloudy-day sunglasses

throwing off weird data when my happy
avatar's heart starts to beat – Hey, whatsup

haemoglobin – what is it that you do again?
I know you can live without this wordage

but there's still something about hand-
rolled keyword dances on a wonder-wall

that bugs on nerve impulses if only you never-
mind … many things are not reckoned by cypher

Damaged Table Service

Poking at the end of a breeze —
does he really believe he's that lucky?
A damaged tray graphs its own rescue.
He has his carpentry, two kids and an
advanced face, practised at the art of
low-budget honesty. She's in every-
one's top five. They all wear glasses.

There is no correlation, he says, between
Hobbits and Somerset. Lifestyle cyclists,
look out for stray cliffs, especially while
managing organizational risk. I can't
believe we missed our targets this month.
At least they agreed to keep poetry to a
minimum and finally supply larger glasses.

we are all just dandy

after exactly fifteen minutes
stuck in an amber analogy
even puking up a rainbow
doesn't feel good anymore

zombie mannequins bear
stigmata they recite poetry –
may the best condiment win
before boredom sets in

some phrases secrete a smell
some words are light as woven
air some details get lost some
words get in the way of day

when the oars dropped over
board i commanded a crab
army in a postdivorce opera
on mount olympus zeus

didn't stand a chance as
i swung on heaven's gate
drooling unstructured data
discharging stickiness and

school uniforms scattered masks
i have to tell you next to whatever
you are beautiful but please make
space this lettuce can't breathe

Fly Me Now

they fly me now *whom I have loved,*
  and as in darkness are
                    – John Milton, Psalm LXXXVIII

Mark that radiant coding and so fill
the space that measures night and day
with slow roasted Melancholy. The re-
calling, sifted and resifted, is spent air.

A deadpool of chocolate fudge edges
submerged in galaxy hops the down-
ward motion sponging out light: you
are unable to unsubscribe at this time.

Happy are those who are glazed in glug,
weighed down with discounts on selected styles,
weighed down with whisperings on wattle blossoms,
weighed down with studious Sophist wit.

Why isn't my engine juicing? Morning
bent northward around the cup-lip yet this
distance, though strung with good intentions,
is cobwebbing my dazed wonder-frame.

Patch up those perforations and put on
your Heraclitus sandals, turtle on through
the shoals, even as data allowance gutters
your stuttering into a Swiss DNA bank.

Happy are those who graze on sea-grass,
mute vessels who churn the cosmic ocean,
their volcanic bloom discharging clips
of dullness into the salty atmosphere.

It's time to meet your continental shelf:
all these legacies of the bottom drawer,
faded foam, ground acorns of hope,
too far out to sea to be writing poetry.

Decompose overall regret into a set
of additive dark regret. In the end, is
only matter triumphant? Rise and rise,
rise amid rage into the pure firmament.

Idle Trade

Mud boggled, painted child
of buzz beside
the graffito.

Check sketch through
broken panes a lazy
sprig of laurel.

Crowd-tagged, lawn reigns
supreme so zip the
jazz already.

Comment streams
convulse, dirt allows
a thought.

Things That Didn't Happen

The freeing scroll, here, come hold the
fooling pole for my share me tragedy her
unparalysed facial muscles made waves
under the ghost of a dignity. She's an aspiring
dolphin trainer doing a broadside hot dog like
Little Bo Peep her Quokka cute face proves
only boring heteronormative white people
deserve love. Crossing into the temporal realm
(temporarily) for frozen margaritas from
a machine, please link me to her wishlist.

Let's back up. I remember when my personality
disorder first spotted me sitting in the front row
at Milan Fashion Week, pen in hand, and Bad
Sugar Daddy knew right away I was destined
to be the next amphibious surplus of the fairy
hole. Welcome to the ugg life, said Daddy,
a house on a golf course, a dog on a skateboard,
shooting wall ducks on your hen's night. Now
my name is Bunnysweat and this is my go-to
cookie face. I know I need to develop a more business-
like attitude towards selling my World's Best Poet Mug
so I asked the fish in my wine glass about branding
this souvenir teaspoon collection. Collections
don't have to have a point, it said, just a like.

Wounded Continuum

The northernmost quantum leapt
over a figure in dust, pennies collect,
I thrash in an envelope. Space your
echoes and solo when the conductor
turns his back, they say, work that pole
until fog from the pool-top rises up to
blank out the bits you don't like.

A sound bite blinks to attention, deposits
its likes along a roll of pulp detached from
a backbone so infinite disaster people keep
sliding down the headlines only to drain out
the inbox. There's nothing quite like dust
gathering on a talking head except that
cabin-full of poems I wrote last summer.

Let's wander off the yellow brick road
together, relax in the backlog and watch
our daily whale chew (whatever it is
whales eat). I wrote so much marbled sky,
accented the word mash with the warmth
of other people's poems, collecting photons
for our nest in this hollow counter-earth.

I Should've Been a Cowboy

When I heard the cows sing, I knew
I should've followed wise Ben Kenobi
beyond the flat-packed mountains.
Besides the adventure, he said, I love
the groupies, groups of them just
grouping along the trail of reviews.

Every now and then I fly back to Brooklyn
on an ancient alien scarab, sucking in wild air
and singing "roll on Kefri, roll on" while I wait
for the next bounce of dark energy. Eventually
comets slide into animal partition glitches and
I return to word prospecting on the digital trail.

The advanced personality disorder of most
poetry groupies doesn't pose much of a threat
says Ben – if you press roses into your pages
and sprinkle them with motivational quotes
they will soon be switching car insurance
and calling things by their real names.

So who's driving this thing? Each new
leaf is a tissue of Biblical phrases like
"shine on, moonshine, shine on". He
who comes from Nowhere said nobody
should be an NPC in their life story – out
here, we're translating irony into energy.

vintage of electronica

(for sw)

set swell to peel,
aqua repeater.

listen to the drops
crisping air with
matched asterisks,
listen to the flow
of the just so.

signal a will in
phrases filtered
through a cell-
splitter at the rate
of continuity.

open
the envelope,
bob moog.

glittered pulses
at the feather edge
of phases sparkle
on undertows em-
bedded with
overload. so
what's next?

hack grandma's
kickstart vibrator
o owl of
widest wild.

Hashtag Poetry

Hashtag poetry, hello eggplant. Open
your mouth and let the words pour out.
Excite a connector, O tag cloud, shake
with racing notes the standing air!

Azure wings, how they fly me now
across each asynchronous benefit zone.
Some prefer full frontal versification to
wallpaper scraps of personal experience.

Your seed feedback, grilled squid. Don't
suffer panic attacks in sidebars alone: mop
up all that feeling, span it across a page,
then space each span with silent spires.

Hashtag booty, hello glue clogs. No-
one appreciates the classics anymore.
Only you can stop the yawning pit of
mediocrity reaching out for my career.

Just as crisp days fill a vacuum, light
enough to room in, so I sift net
detritus to witness the rivers inside:
provide whatever images you think fit

but don't discard my yo-yo. An empty
mailbox is split by an echo, doubt
scatters the capacity to be consistent.
Anyway, thanks for reaching out.

Have You Been Serviced Recently?

Chat, flirt and calibrate – our servicing strategy
works with backspace. I ordered an Angel Sanctuary
covered in a Thousand Cherry Blossoms but
the Sons of Spandex tapped the wrong button.
"Cookie dough" is not a euphemism. Fine then,
I will participate in this terminology.

When my scenario progressed into disrupt
the app logs exposed a sensitive defect.
Why buy the cow when you can have
100 percent hotness in cowboy boots?
SOS? Seriously? Only if you get a
refund on that plastic surgery already.

Bad mall food decisions often happen
while you're waiting for servicing.

At Clark Coolidge Cave

On maybe meanings, pixelated coral.
Behind my puncture there's a hollow
data lode. This is wishful loafness.

An unsettling strum releases
veins of ink, catchable throat
sounds, the energy in cleavage.

Metric teeth, stripped of alchemy.
No crow's feet to compensate for
forgetting the riff of the Solar Kingdom.

Release the restlessness, Keith Jarrett.
Release my relaxing option anxiety.
The bubbling up rebuilds an animal.

Of meaning groping. Fingering bare
by the bulb's drain. Will you reveal
your niche before the next ice age?

Tug of asterisks at the tomb steps,
blunted wants cased in a short spectrum.
The cave is an alignment of crushed silence.

Hair by Ballerina in a Rush

Overpriced pink flamingo won't oppose feminist reforms
so long as she can remain living in her own champagne
bubble of perfection. Listen up, your beige stuff is just
not going to cut it anymore. This is a shout-out to the
frown, the eyebrow arch, the hair by ballerina in a rush.

Someone let the non-knowers know that Chill Pussy is
doing the Hotline Bling. Someone tell her she's heading
into Real Life Mary Sue territory and that is SOOOOO
not a good thing. Say, has anyone got any laurels? Any
frosting that once adorned the heads of Shepherdesses?

Inspired by a classic Voltaire quote about avoiding
synthetic wigs, Corn Husk Doll stopped decoding
postal codes. Computation is embarrassing, it said,
like peeling away layers of an onion, only the tears
are real and the plastic polymers don't blow dry.

Imagine my bok choy after a bad blow dry and you're
almost there. Distressed denim means innovation, it is
not a special effect. OK, the fauxhawk was to pump sales,
the hair by medication unfixed, empty trays everywhere.
I can't believe I pulled myself out of a puddle for this.

Once the Latin speeches ended, Creamy Mob Wife Barbie
stained my iris dancing to Viva Las Vegas. A future event
causes a photon to decide its past. Three cheers for pap-flipping
flamingos, said Ball Park Frank, several poems ago. Nothing
says classy, added Real Life Mary Sue, like one brand head to toe.

Breakfast with Frank

It's not quite snowing when eggwhites
enter from the diamond window door
and Grade A Fancy whipped cream
confidence and stainless steel shine
aren't enough to unsmudge my ruminations:
Do only women have legs on TV?
Do the French know about the toast
they left at the next table? Do the Greeks
behind the counter know where
they hid the Parthenon key?

Outside, everyone seems to have a direction,
no one pauses to absorb the squeaky clean
House of Lever, maybe they're already
thinking about what's for lunch. Not

me, I'm still at the Stone last night,
nerves twitching on John Zorn's vibrato
fat and wide like a melancholy duck
stuttering to work in camouflage pants
a long-necked matzo ball solo on
a turkey bacon flight to the last westbound
whiskey bar in Hell's Kitchen deep in
the stacks at the Strand Bookstore somewhere
between History and Philosophy when
time crystalized and you were there.

Then a guy sits down at the counter
and looks just like any other guy,
no one even notices that he looks
the same as the guy who just left.

Don't You Get It?

It's possible, rather than I *get* it. Tacit
moods creep in until treatment becomes
available. Is this a preview of the shaping
image, smooth brow, out there, somewhere?

Computation is an embarrassing remainder
of our abandoned commune. Remember when
we met in that first blind data? Performance,
you said, is all the things you are. You are

the petrified word-world as dusk gutters,
too much matter to overcome desire. Sense,
meet my precious little chit of words, my
condensed substitute, your glancing blow.

master blend

an elect chunk
across the bass

her lightly salted
sister's lanyard

dipped in hair

burnt corn rarely
aligns with my energy

an insolvent
language enlightens

this thickening

moon lust
on a whole rest

filtering down
to earth

now

another armory show

I

fake moustache on that emu.
scrolling through ensuite pics,
choosing the right bowl is hard.

II

This morning while I was meditating, the universe sent me a vision
about using all my savings to travel to India and teach yoga to
the impoverished children there, and I think my future self will
always regret it if I don't follow my dreams.

III

clean bulk monk don't
gummy warm to cryptic
humblebrag no more.

after that last haircut lust
we are no longer permitted
to comment on operational matters.

push the taste button if you must but
please don't touch the plumbing
i need to breathe

IV

This might be a reference that will only work for those of you
who are parents or who are especially into animated films.

V

fake moustache
on that grass mud horse.
people want to see celebrity.

VII

a rose is
not a random word.

a clam is
always happy.

Calculus Flowers

Only false species leak key circuitry,
shiver at sunlight, gum up in front of
wrinkle, tombs and worms. In the future,
all this squishy stuff in the middle will
be more natural, frictionless and nothing
will feel like filling in a form anymore.

When a laser cores the rose, happy people
will stop tonguing and make words scroll.
When the sky is toilet-bowl blue, scraped data
from the extractor will inspire more eyebrows.
When Kurma the tortoise retires, the Bubble
Guppies will shower him with shiny ka-ching.
Only then will our addiction to calculus flowers
stop its positive impact on emotional outcomes.

Smells Like Perfectly Peachy

I

If what I wear doesn't creative for you,
invent your own religion of indifference.

Even though most people think of poetry as
uncooked cookie dough or mental celery, I have
so much admires for the guys who bottled its
Modern Spirit. Like jazz, poems just keep going,
smoke-hollowed in exposed flame rhythms,
shaping an image not yet swimming in screens.

As you can probably tell, my many photos of petals
in the Paris Metro were inspired by a trip to Mexico.

II

Flicking your own bean is not a terrible
life choice so long as it's freshly buttered.

I had to switch the flattening machine to snooze
to compose a poem for Miss Tiara in Manila. Her
Pink Lyric theorem bubbled at my cognitive plug-in
but my aimer cradles a full contempt bucket list.
These days, cupcakes and cashmere will elevate
subscribers more than a bag of lit conference swag.

Each leg lifting over belly, sewing machine tattoo,
my libido of faulty gender lifted bubbles over.

III

Created in the Czech Republic, her diamond studded
tiara is exempt from tax so you know it's expensive.

Thanks anyway for the entertainment, thanks for the
fabric scraps held together with staples, it's what every
red carpet needs. When I was doing the Pretzel Twist
I know I let my mental celery fall by the wayside. It's
back there somewhere, caught on the fame wire
beside the aphorisms that changed the world.

No consolation, but here are some cookies.
Hey, I don't lift everyone like this.

Screen Scrape

Reset the lyric clock
these beaded microbes
winking at the brim
should eliminate the
sound of broken people.

Like stats chopped into graphs.
Like kids eating paint chips.
Like colon tea to detoxify your body.
Like liking looking but not licking.

Don't you find it frustrating following people
for inspiration and they just stop inspiring?

Also,
Thor rules.

Undone in London

That night, Diana appeared to me and
told me to sail to a sea-girt land. That
would take too long, said I, can't I fly?

I: Diana thrust out, Paul installed

Exciting reflections on my journey (so far!):
I began by crossing the road at the gatehouse
by the Spaniard's Inn where, once upon a time,
giants posted selfies. In their ruffled pirate shirts
and velvet jackets, they wrote odes to the last princess.
In those days, windows were smaller, which added
to the general vibe of decadent moodiness. Today,
you can sit on a dark pew and a Russian waitress will
bring you confit duck on a lentil mash and an oaken ale.
That's when my opposable thumb clicked on Diana
in the bath, keeping it PG for a while, until, like an enabler,
I added a Cannes manfur wig for luck. My quest was to
restore her antiquity or found another Troy, whichever
came first. What has been reported thus far differs from
what actually occurred. Such as the incident at the deer
park, all the squishy stuff in the middle years and the
secret devotions the bog man whispered in my ear.

Back on the road, Paul couldn't see Diana standing
in her own moonlight, a ladderback chair alone on the
heath, talking to my nightingale. Not that he would've
believed any of this anyway. When he's not posting his
travel pics, he's totally "noping" everyone's messy unicorn
dreams, their Lofty Ambitions in Forests and Streams. Looking
through his beer glass dimly, bald Paul's dome dominates the room.
So drink up. Here's a stag's head, photoshopped onto my body.

II: The Art of St Bart

Paul isn't the only one who's been to India. Phil's buddy
Bart was over there long before it was fashionable to be
washed up on an island off Sicily, left in a crush behind
the wire or trying to board a train in Budapest. Tear-
gassed in Calais, Bart was flayed on the razor wire,
his skin lifting from its muscle and bone in an effort
to achieve an anatomically minimal form of existence.
But this was lost in the pub hubbub, weathered edges,
foamy tops on beams of warm imagination. I dreamt of
a Caribbean vacation, of tanning without any lotion, of
old growth oak cycling through the seasons. It's no
wonder Blake looked in on his way past from Old Wyldes,
Bart posing with his skin draped across a shoulder like a toga,
the panicked crowd, assuming he was an alien, threw pint
glasses and attacked him with cutlery. Clearly, casting out
demons was out of the question. If this was the Bay Area
he could start a cult but Bart's lonely journey ended in a
poetry composter. Meanwhile, Paul patented another genetic
estate (he was a lawyer) before he too felt persecuted.

Diana appears from time to time as a polite mist that obscures
the Brutalist city. Assorted straws bypass the anthology. Bart
reputedly helps whatever poet can't stand their distortion pill.
And me? With so many avatars to swipe at, I was just happy to be
part of it, a witness to past greatness. Best of all, I saw how
parkour made the city a stage again, just as Shakespeare predicted.

Hey, I Sent You a Poem, Did You Get It?

Easter sale discount code
the revelations came slow

She moistened her plasma
so it looks nice for Jesus

Watermelon and kale
are both doing so well

Nothing you can say will
take away my glitter trail

Give Up Your Information

Calm me, chili ramen, calm my
cosmological rage! Yet more asterisk
kisses beside a honey-customized sunrise.
Yet more minimalist forests and fields.
Yet more foot follows eyeball juice.

Line of hindsight, make moist
while the pudding cools. Did
you feel that tiny earthquake?
My oatcake, loaded with cheese
and cucumber, buckled in half.

Men clutching clipboards hedge
against muddy footprints in an
ancient white cube. I aspire
to spiral within its steeple but
this app inhibits habitual script.

Come, look at my phone. See,
these are not persons of quality.
Down with brilliance fashioned
into words! They have a system
now for coding mental celery.

Cumberland Lodge

give not way
the key to detail
a number under
the table by
the charming
everyone likes
to lick the icing
off the ceiling.

earwax on catgut

spits seltzer on cat

my troubles doth
discompose me

one only has to
rotate a portrait
to see the landscape.

greases the polite

many layers make
up a lacquer Japan
(she curates shoes
on Instagram)

*feels better now that 19th century
working women finally have agency*

even periwigs
I have none

clutches bloomers

no one likes
a bashful sun.

give not way
not even
after pudding.

Animal Modes of Melancholia

As the chance inheritor of a language parasite,
I can tell you these are definitely angels' tears,
not mine. Their serotonin transporters must be
malfunctioning and now, like a Bhutanese
refugee, ecstasy has finally caught up with me.

But this dark weight is not on the amphibian
within. He's a capable turtle, adept at activating
Reward Mood Memory in the correct order. He's
just tired at the moment, resting in the stem of
consciousness, speechless, fingering at a screen.

This distillation might inhibit the reabsorption
of serotonin as tear drops possess overtones.
Even Buddhists believe all information about
former configurations are stored "in a cloud".

Just Make It

Putting aside the frosted fields and ambient
larksong along hedge edges, some words
just don't get along. A crop of stunted
kindling swims in screens, its soft attention
mediating between one pub and the next.

Slow food moves, slowly. Heritage rises
around a stone prefix, concealing leaks
in rental realism and a bell addiction.

Even as prose tosses another character
into the copyright flattening machine,
I'm restalking Jack's single origin beans,
flinting at chipped theses in the hope that this
fine English mist might burst the decimal club.

All Breakfast's Footnotes

Come, feel my bonsai.
Smooth ale, East Anglian mud.
I have designed bones for
you, buried them in a bog.

Pleasant butter brushes on
Heritage. Heritage encodes
statistics. The stats app stalled.
Are you listening, mini pony?

World of Hair Extensions

Unlock a bicycle skull pulse til
this metal saint ascends. There's
still an uneasy blank between us.

The burnt era kept returning, sink
and overload before I could insert
words into the confidence socket.

This thicket is dense.

Unlock a catastrophic look and
interrogate the same pulse again,
then release another liked shadow.

An extension waves, perhaps it's
a believable performance after all.
Handlebars make great moustaches.

Did you like my liked shadow?

Unlock the cloud combination to
cover your sun, my vain attempt
at liking is only kicking up ash.

I know there's been breakage but we *will*
open that gourmet popcorn shop one day,
as soon as I peel this wrinkle mask off.

Here, Let Me Open This for You

Most of my data is dark and unstructured but
what you see is
                        eggs on eggs in a sea of cheese.

Live analytics indicates it's time to pluck ripe
clusters and repost them to the Museum of MeMeme.

O clouds unfold
                        these deposits of metric litter
blinked in Morse Code:
                        Such Perfection,
wrapped in half-price decorations from Party City!
                                No one likes opinionated eggs.

So I heard you climbed Theory Mountain beyond the Word Perilous,
and finally bid adieu to the fake Eiffel Tower, so good for you. I'm still
on the gondola ride in a Macau casino, pouring a stream of taxpayers' tears
into a crystal goblet with one hand while typing poems about doubt
on this typewriter with the other. And who cares about bearded critics?

I know, right?
            Sploosh
                        Damn. I'm all splashed out.

Auto-Doubt

the shell emits the right sounds in
the right order that pass as words
but only express the passage of
nothingness after auto-delete.

sag under-eyes shelter a surplus,
they gutter wonder into the sink.

lust snacks between squalls,
love calculates the threat then
grants the latest last straw.

fragility enters its shallow parody
of animal melancholia to repress the
foaming, to regulate signal intensity.

we are mostly water, she said, like
cucumbers. cucumbers with anxiety.

Poetry as Fake Therapy

Poetry, perpetually out picking up milk
from the store, was always gone so long
I got used to black coffee. In fact, I soon
came to like it more than white coffee.

And, who wants poetry with their coffee,
anyway? Isn't life complicated enough?

Her Name is Echo and She Always Answers Back

I woke up like this, an ex-poet knitting socks
by the pool, on copper and rose gold cushions,
shaving, sucking in, filtering the density of light
beside the Diet Coke of Evil. Evil swerves easily
away, as though to protect what it advertises. A
flipbook of thickening makeup hooks onto a pupil,
a white bikini disappears up your glazed butt,
Japanese screens hide that awful avocado feature
wall. I love that we have these memories. Hello, I'm
by the pool, there's better lighting here and these aviators
highlight the extra burden of representation. Keeping
a low profile at the Trevi Fountain, all eyes on Rome,
you get the feel better as the light faded. Only a little
water keeps us apart. And keep the coins coming.

Here's me at Treblinka. This is not my real hair, of
course! My eyes fixated, typo-squatting, the inner
life of my hair adhering to a face. Faces don't easily
turn, nor do they lie flat, but you can choose a back-
ground and plenty of other people who aren't "vaguely
Middle Eastern women". My confidence is such that
everyone really thought I was a Nobel Prize winning
author. I don't think you ever reach a magical point in
your life where your cup of self-exploration is full.
I love doing photo shoots and having memories.
They have methods to purify the fat and graft it onto
an image. It doesn't even have to look good, just
create a buzz. There is no rap career, I clearly said
"Vermeer". Third time I've apologized this week.

My thumb at rest, all I see is an empty bathroom,
black strips of empowerment or judgement. My
journey of recovery began on this yoga mat,
it followed the tile trail, scrolling so far and yet
this is definitely the wrong party. My cupcakes
are almost like a Renaissance thing, a painting,
a proxy for social interaction. Getting ahead on
next season's look sounds a lot easier than
sending computers to India. Here's me pinching the
Taj Mahal at the pointy end of its garlic bulb head.
Sometimes I can't pull up the blinds. I know
this poem would be better off without me. So
many memories splashed out in the dark, kissing
a pillow. So here's my best body, in parts.

Not that I'm following you but we have a nice
bathroom, roomy and empty, perfect for performing
Beckett monologues in spite of the tennis. All that
introspective dialogue and intensity are merely distraction
from the rounded reflecting surface that divides our
investment between originality and its digital wash.
Wait, who are you getting ready for? Clutching at
pearls, reflecting on the multitudes who've used
this bathroom before you, each one leaving
a little bit of themselves behind. Deflecting all
advances, are you a goddess in human form or
a bundle of dispositions continually being reborn?
All these private moments, I hope you'll remember
me. But this not my book. It's just for staging.

Afterword:
How I Came to Write Certain of These Verses

People often ask me how I came to write certain of these verses. Of course, *why* is easier to explain so perhaps I should start there. Like all poets, I wanted to express myself in my own voice, win prize money and receive fan mail. Believe it or not, that was the easy part. *How* I achieved that was not only difficult but difficult to explain. So, from the beginning...

The Moment of Conception
Keratin is a — nay, *the* — structural material that makes up the outer layer of human skin. It's tough, insoluble, but also permeable, and when your keratin touches someone else's keratin something miraculous happens. I imagine silicone filler below the surface might affect this. Also, losing Pluto was a personal blow. And this isn't just about me. Many people — a whole generation, I suspect — grew up with a solar system map comprising nine planets and were shocked when, in 2006, the International Astronomical Union voted against Pluto's status as a planet. Overnight, we were down to eight planets and some icy spheres that no one talked about. While school children today are at peace with this revised solar system, there's clearly an important lesson here. Finally, the 2003 discovery of Hobbits — not, as you might expect, in New Zealand, but in Indonesia — unsettled the other end of my evolutionary scale. They say it's a new species but it's hard to know what to believe anymore.

The Digital Vernacular
You might remember from my first book, *Happy Avatar,* that I often put on an *accent* when talking on the phone or texting. Although many people think this *funny* or *phoney,* it's simply *my way of fitting in.* In this wonderful world of connectedness, I live what's called an "open source lifestyle". Open source selves are difficult to spot (liking is easier than looking, after all). Most of us have nothing to say but are saying it in interesting ways. In this vibrant linguist mist we inhabit, curious

juxtapositions emerge. Celebrities like Little Bo Peep and the Sons of Spandex share their thoughts not only on "big" issues such as climate change and capitalism but also share their exfoliation regimes. So many people make interesting comments. Unfortunately, others, such as Pacman, have no respect for proper punctuation. The world of data harvesting is abounding with ampersands. No word is firm.

How I Came to Move to Paraguay

Many Australian poets are fond of changing into their superhero costumes in a telephone box. Sadly, they all try and jam into a single box. That's when the fighting starts. And it's getting worse because, in the 21st century, telephone boxes are almost impossible to find. That's why, about a decade ago, I moved out of Ramsay Street for good and migrated to Paraguay. I found I had a lot more room to move and, in South America, no one cares what you wear. But I like to visit Australia from time to time. Sometimes, when I'm camping or at the beach, I hear plain-spoken poetry floating over the palings and wonder if I'm missing out on something. Thankfully, being a poet in Paraguay isn't much of a commitment.

Men with Selfish Centres

These guys like to claim that invisible hands do all the work. Don't believe it. They employ smart people to write the algorithms for them.

So Why Won't Nature Smile?

I realize that it's been getting warmer but I'm not complaining because I like wearing shorts and going to the beach. Of course, that's not to say that working towards more sustainable syntax isn't one of my life goals. As a part – I grant you, *tiny* – part of nature, I sometimes find it hard to get along with other parts. Like lawns, for instance. Or this unsettling fact: in Florida, there are more pink plastic flamingos than real ones. As a famous philosopher once said (and I can attest to this from personal experience), "poetry is not a useful gardening tool", especially when you're installing Astroturf.

So Much Variety

Poetry is something people only read at weddings and funerals. Therefore, if you're interested in writing poetry it's good to start with verse that is either *happy* or *sad*. In-between verse is not at all popular so it's best to stick to these Big Two (as we call them in the trade). I tried for a while, but I grew up watching variety shows like the Muppets so naturally I'm drawn to lots of different bits and pieces all working together yet each one significant and shiny in its own way. And everyone knows weddings and funerals are bland and predictable.

That's why I became a DJ.

Acknowledgements & Thanks

Poems from this collection have been previously published in the following journals: *VLAK*, *Cordite*, *Soluble Edge*, *Australian Poetry Journal*, *OZ Burp*, *West Wind Review*, *Have Your Chill* and *Otoliths*.

Shout-outs to Louis Armand, Pete Spence, Ann Vickery, Gig Ryan and Michael Farrell for support and thoughts. And gratitude to enablers Sarah Hall in Brooklyn and Grace Lees-Maffei in East Anglia.

Thanks to Ann Vickery and David Musgrave for making this book a reality.